THE FABER EASY-PLAY KEYBOARD SERI

Play Romantic Vienna

arranged for easy keyboard
by Daniel Scott

FABER MUSIC

Contents

© 1989 by Faber Music Ltd
First published in 1989 by Faber Music Ltd
3 Queen Square, London WC1N 3AU
Music drawn by Sambo Music Engraving
Cover design and typography by John Bury
Printed in England

Austrian Hymn

JOSEPH HAYDN

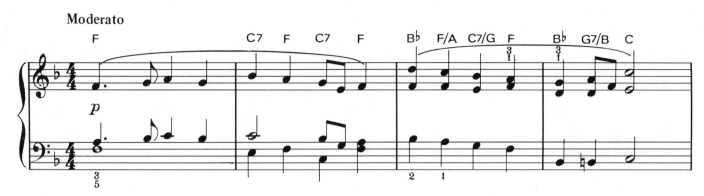

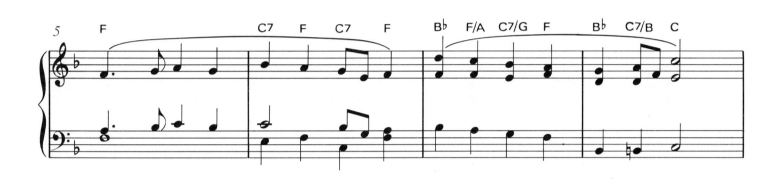

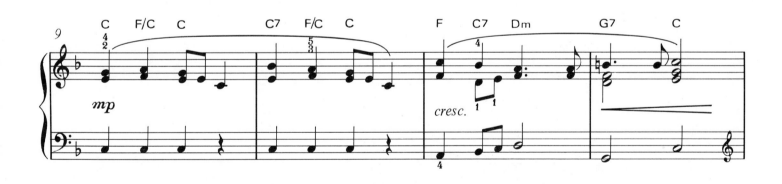

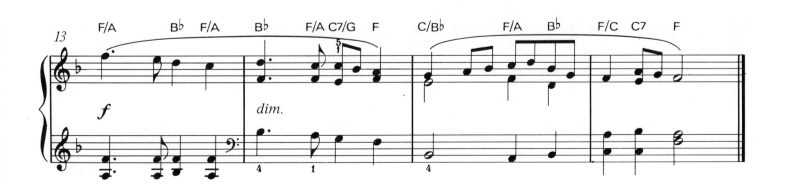

Theme from Piano Concerto K.467

WOLFGANG AMADEUS MOZART

Theme from Clarinet Concerto

WOLFGANG AMADEUS MOZART

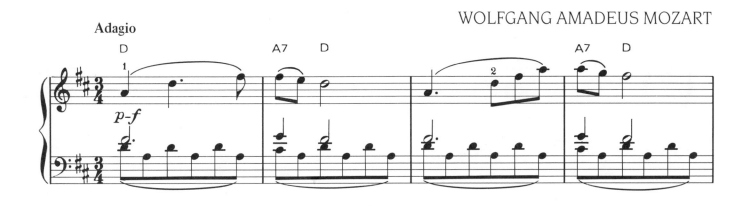

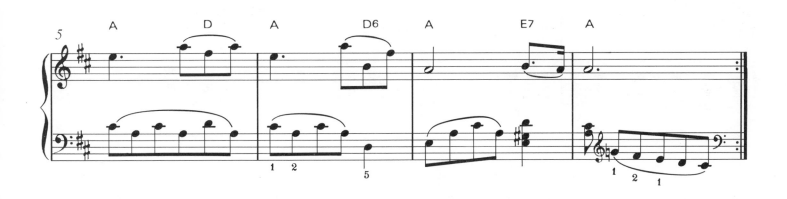

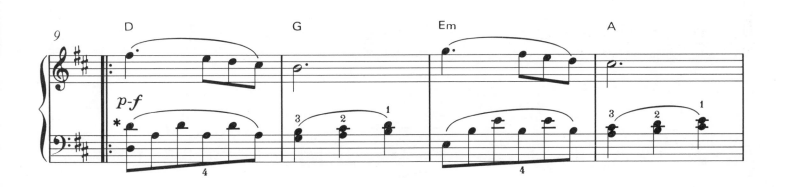

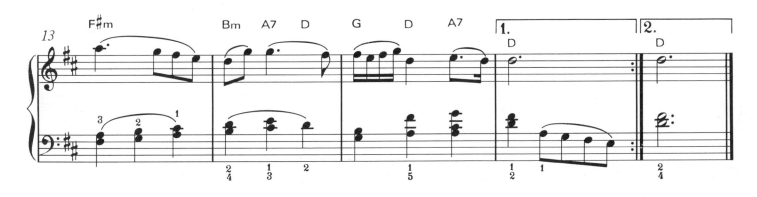

✱ Upper D first time, lower D second time.

Theme from Symphony No. 40

WOLFGANG AMADEUS MOZART

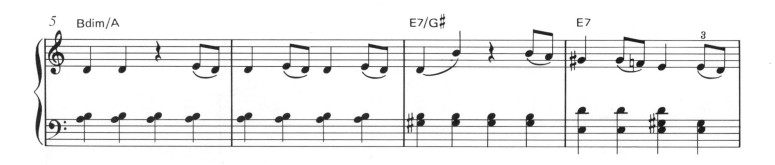

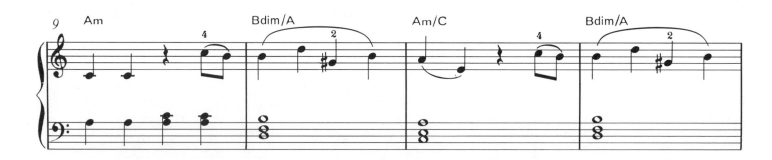

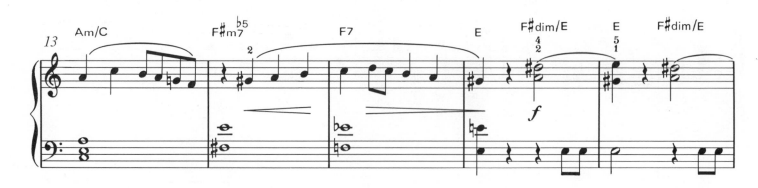

Romanze from Piano Concerto K.466

WOLFGANG AMADEUS MOZART

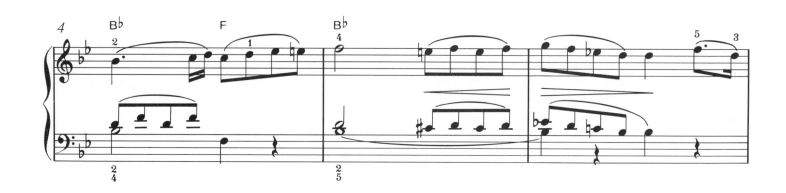

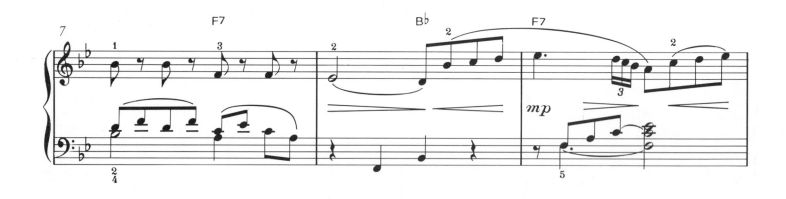

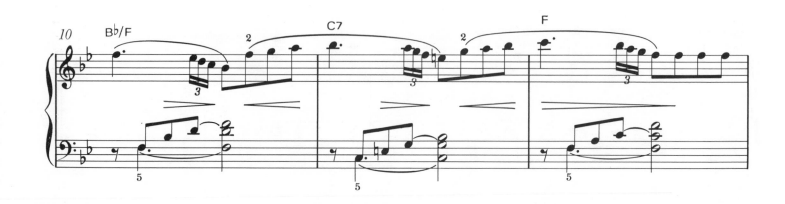

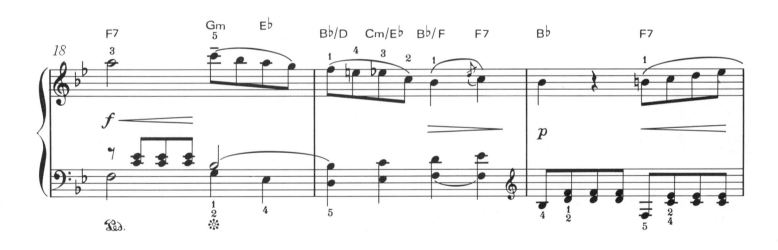

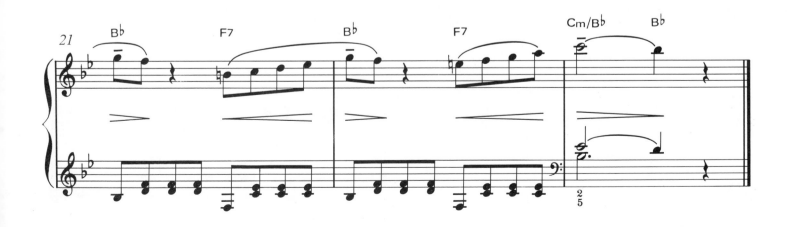

Romanze from *Eine kleine Nachtmusik*

WOLFGANG AMADEUS MOZART

Ode to Joy from Symphony No. 9

LUDWIG VAN BEETHOVEN

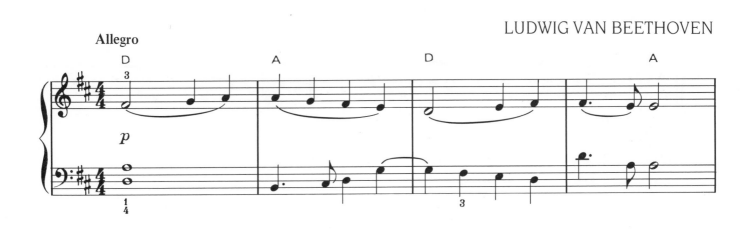

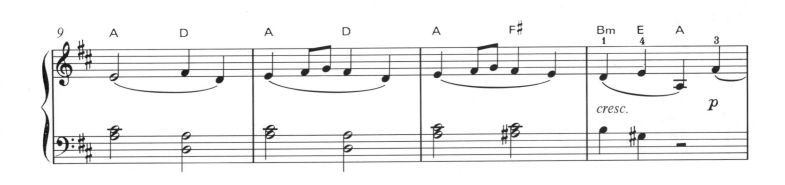

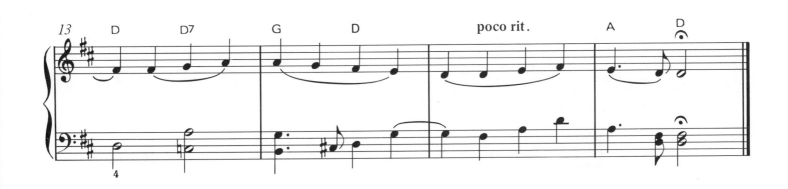

Theme from 'Moonlight' Sonata

LUDWIG VAN BEETHOVEN

Romance in F

LUDWIG VAN BEETHOVEN

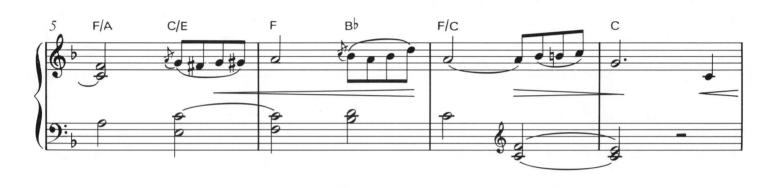

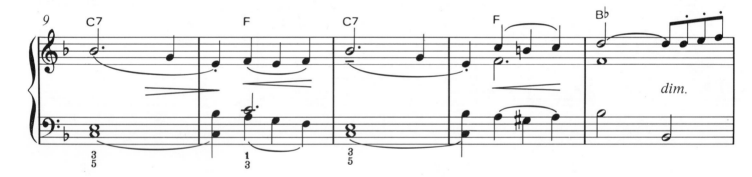

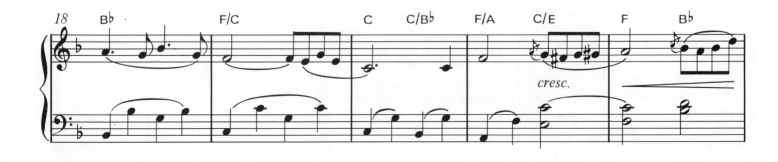

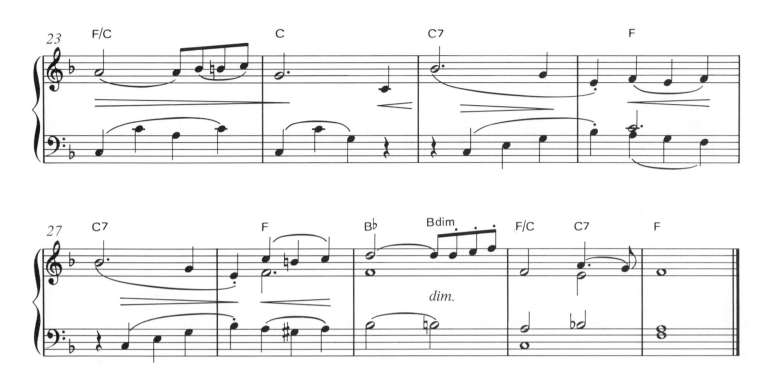

Theme from Piano Concerto No. 5

LUDWIG VAN BEETHOVEN

Theme from Symphony No. 7

LUDWIG VAN BEETHOVEN

Minuet in G

LUDWIG VAN BEETHOVEN

Impromptu Op. 142 No. 3

FRANZ SCHUBERT

Theme from 'Death and the Maiden'

FRANZ SCHUBERT

Theme from Piano Trio No. 2

FRANZ SCHUBERT

Theme from 'Unfinished' Symphony

FRANZ SCHUBERT

Marche Militaire

FRANZ SCHUBERT

Serenade

FRANZ SCHUBERT

Theme from 'St. Anthony' Variations

JOHANNES BRAHMS

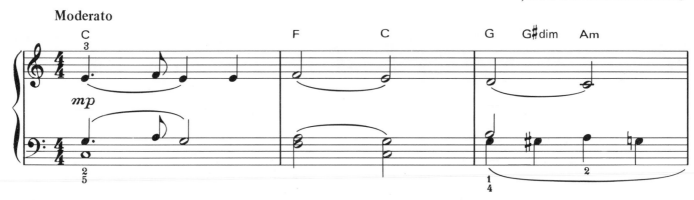

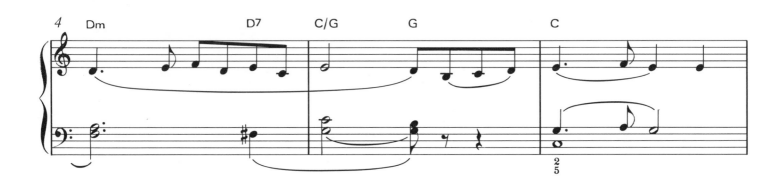

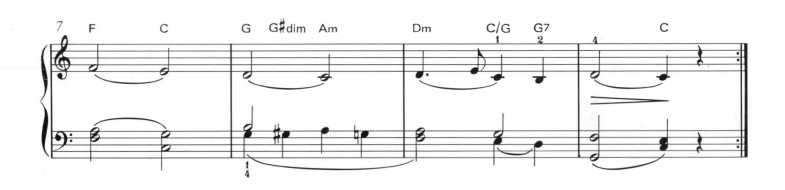

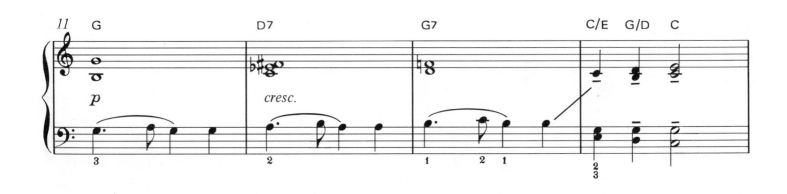

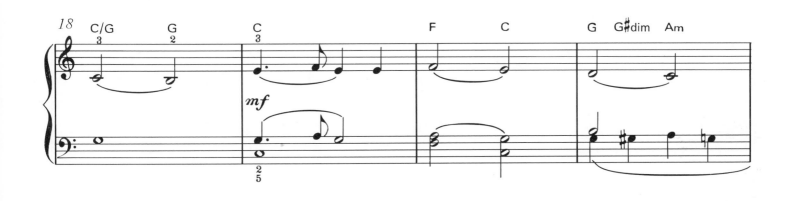

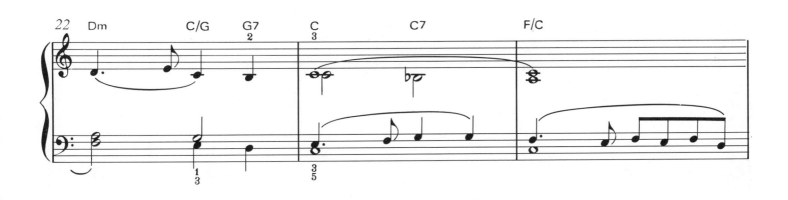

Theme from Violin Concerto

JOHANNES BRAHMS

Lullaby

JOHANNES BRAHMS

Hungarian Dance No. 5

JOHANNES BRAHMS

Theme from Symphony No. 1

JOHANNES BRAHMS

Waltz 'The Blue Danube'

JOHANN STRAUSS

Waltz 'Tales from the Vienna Woods'

JOHANN STRAUSS

'Emperor' Waltz

JOHANN STRAUSS

Adagietto from Symphony No. 5

GUSTAV MAHLER

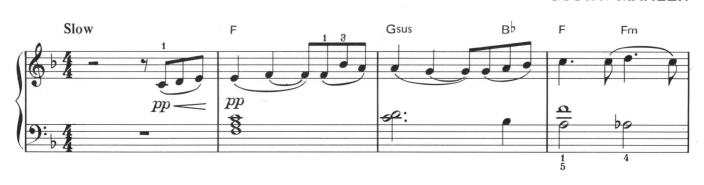

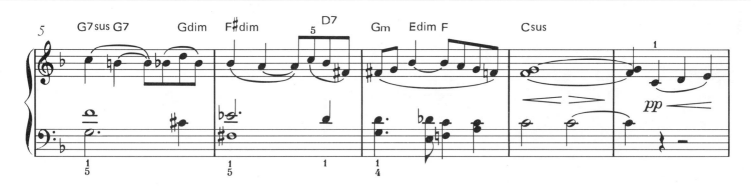

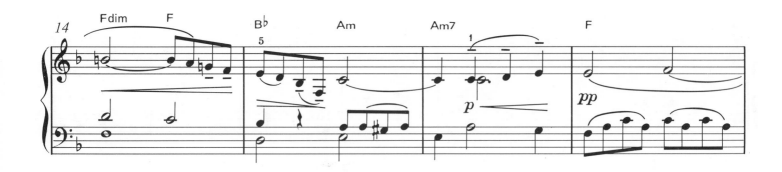

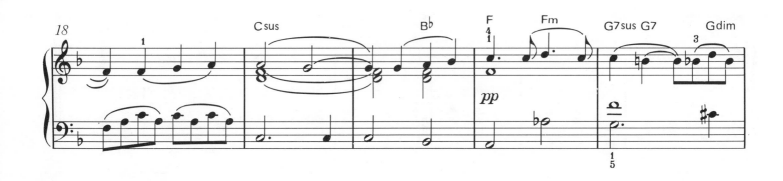

Theme from Finale of Symphony No. 1

GUSTAV MAHLER

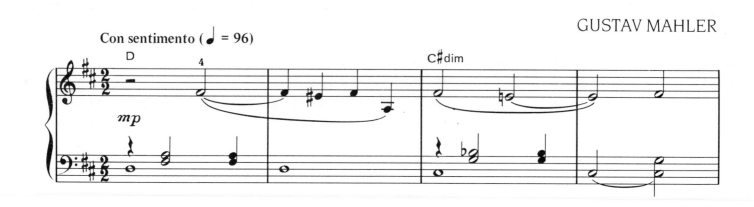

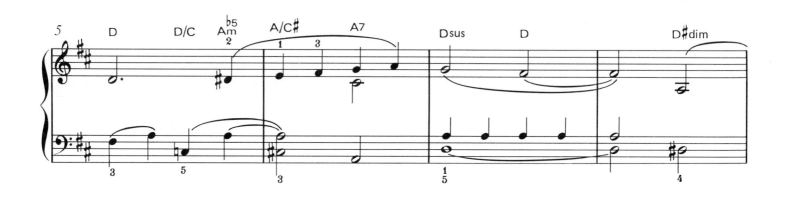

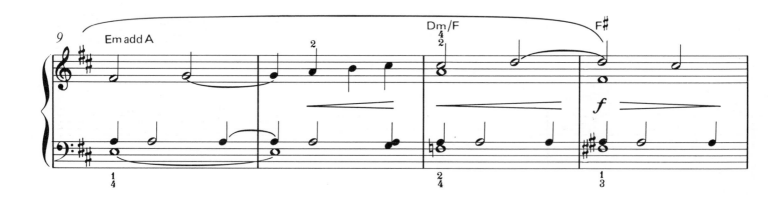

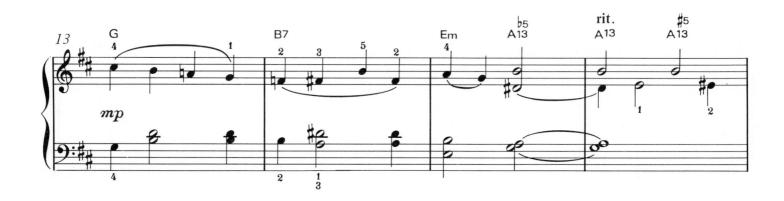

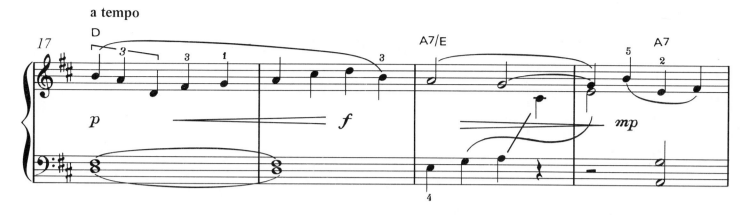

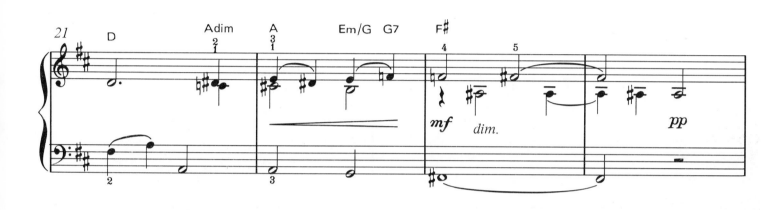

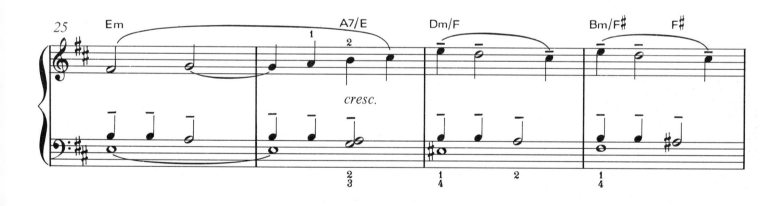

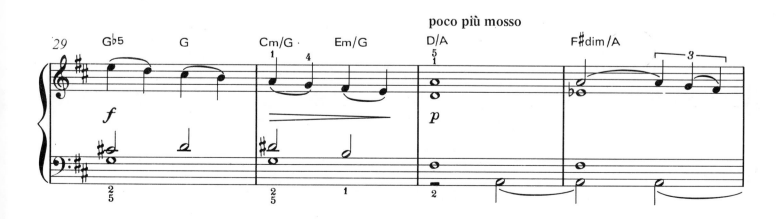

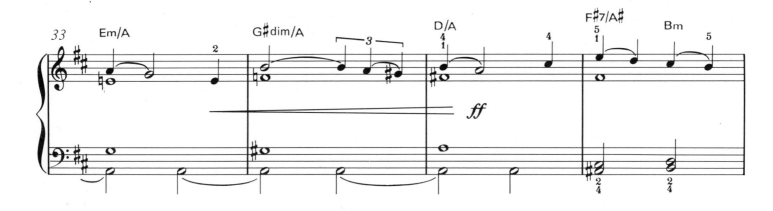

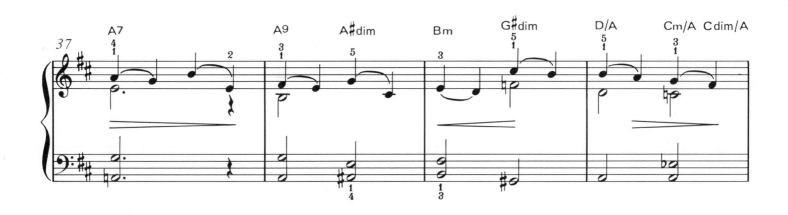

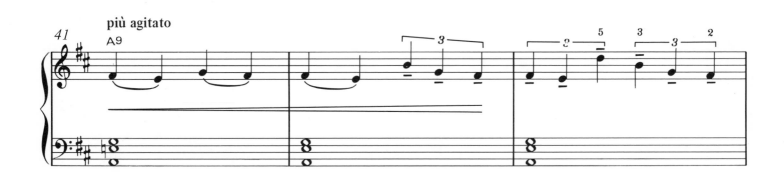

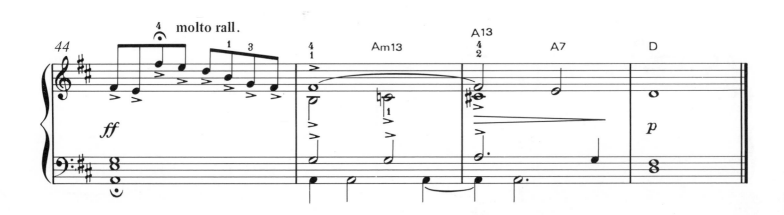